Story & art by

Karl Beckstrand

BIG
BLACK
Seed

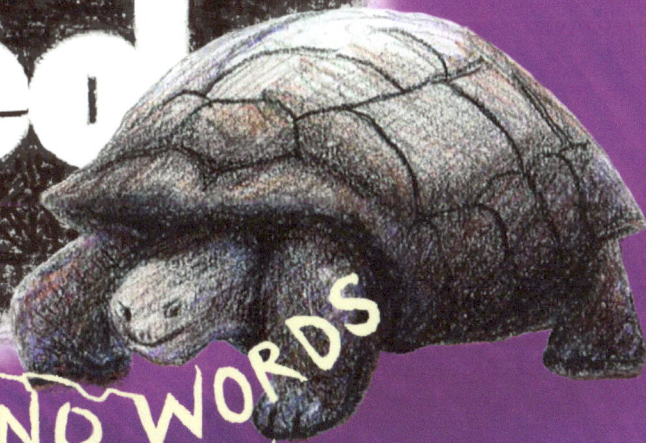

A BOOK WITH NO WORDS

Big Black Seed: A Book With No Words

For Luiz Antonio

Story and illustrations by **Karl Beckstrand,** Copyright © 2025
Premio Publishing & Gozo Books, Midvale, UT, USA
LCCN: 2025935015
ISBN: 978-1951599256

Tell the story and FIND the tortoise, cat, pigs, birds, cricket, worm, pill bug, centipede, spider, and butterfly (also: a seed on every spread)

Get all 4 Stories Without Words (hard/soft/ebook series).
ORDER direct or via major distributors.
FREE multicultural ebooks, online SECRETS, lesson plans & book bundles:

KB Kids World Books **KidsWorldBooks.com**

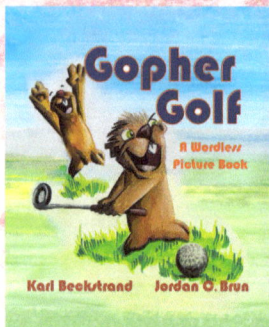

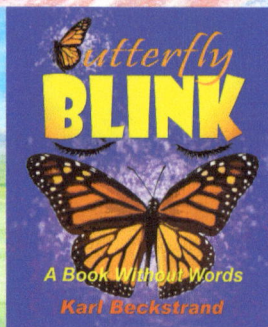

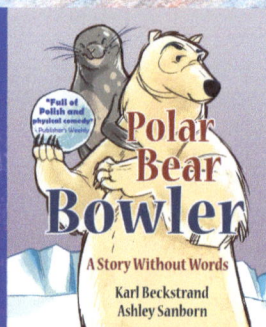

Gopher Golf
A Wordless Picture Book
Karl Beckstrand Jordan O. Brun

utterfly BLINK
A Book Without Words
Karl Beckstrand

"Full of Polish and physical comedy"
Polar Bear Bowler
A Story Without Words
Karl Beckstrand
Ashley Sanborn

MORE FUN

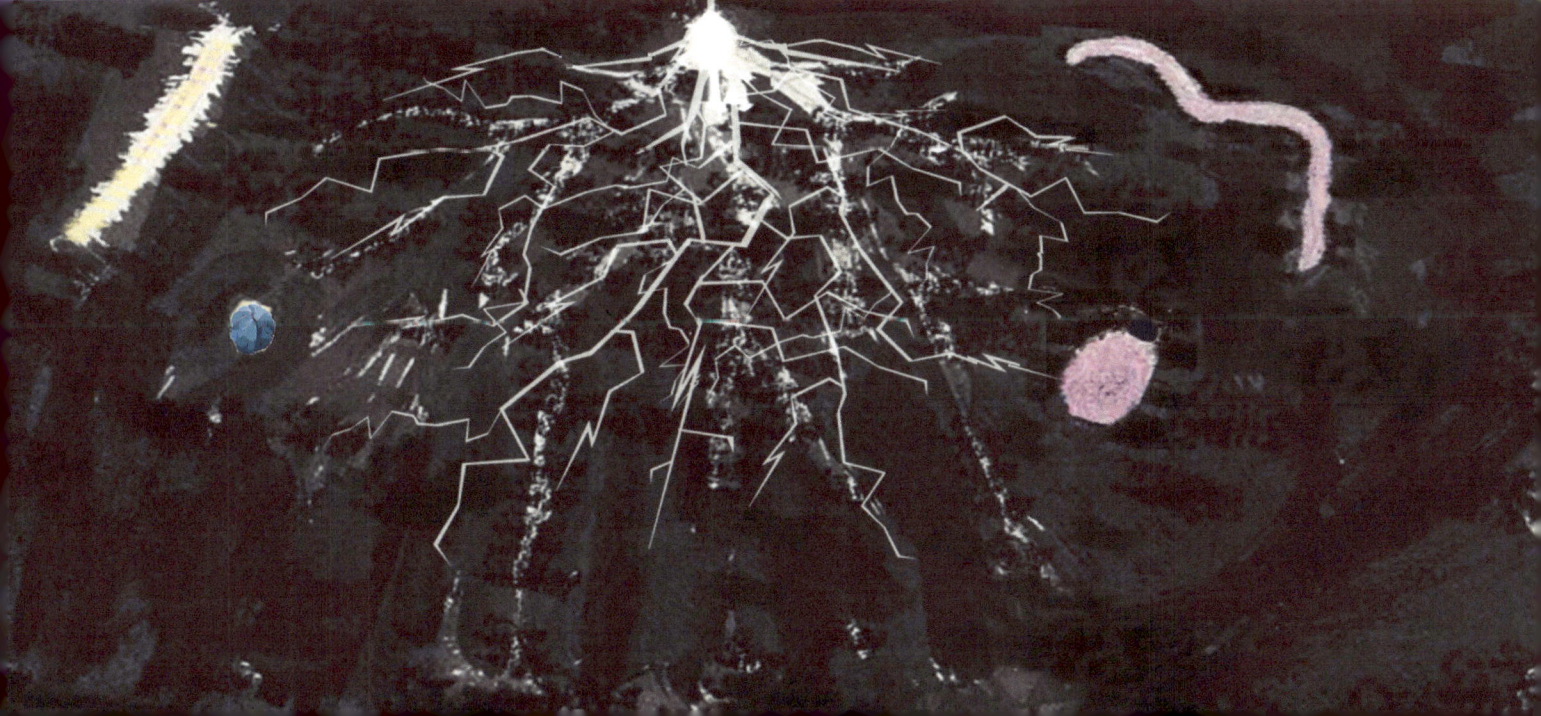

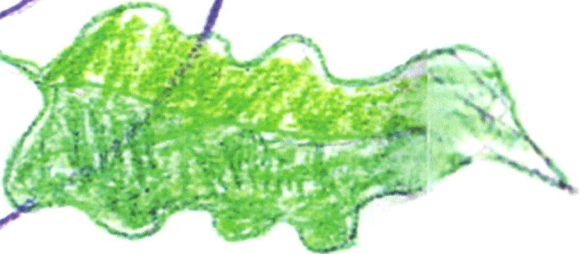

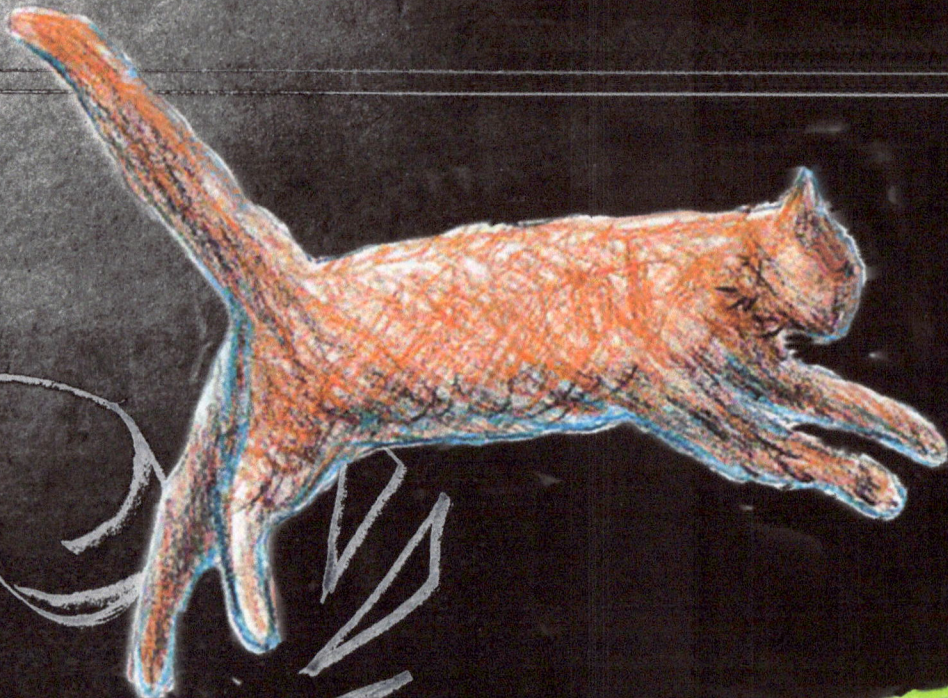

Who are the "3 sisters"?
Find out in online story secrets:

KidsWorldBooks.com

	Animal/Pet	Mystery	Food	TongueTwist/Career	Sports/Outdoors
Humor	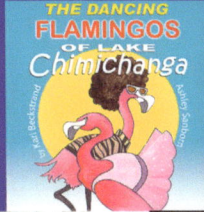		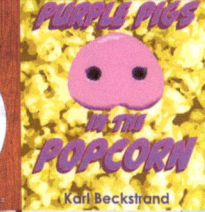	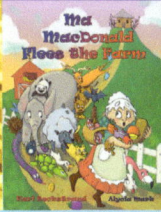	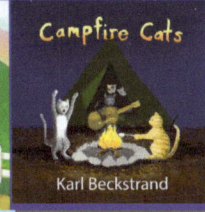
Nonfiction	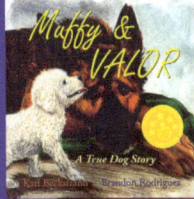	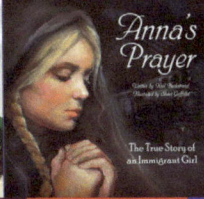	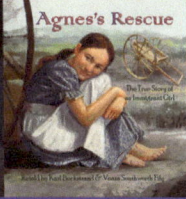	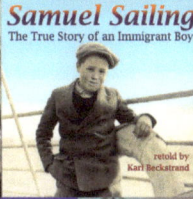	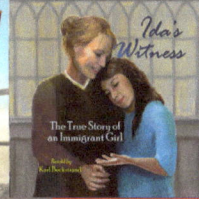
Teen/YA	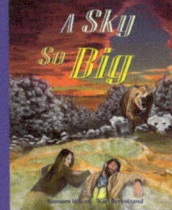	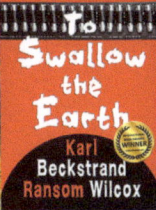	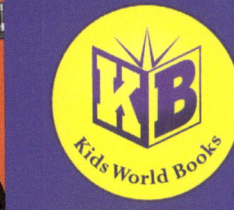		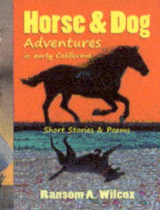
Wordless		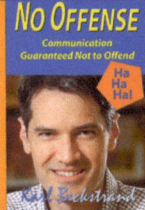	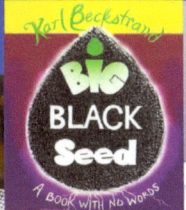	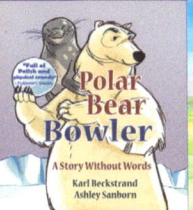	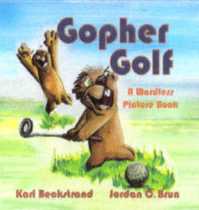
Spanish	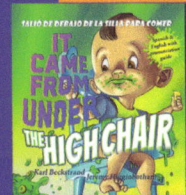	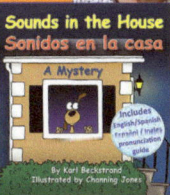			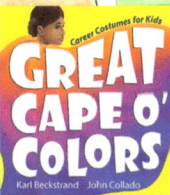 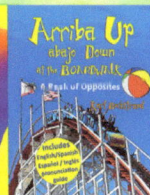
STEM		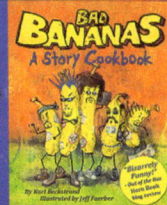	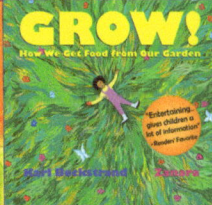	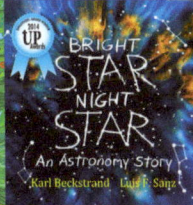	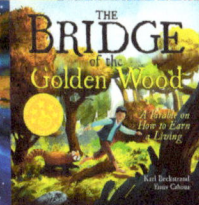

Amazon, Apple, Baker & Taylor, Barnes & Noble, Biblio, Brodart, ChildrensPlusInc, EBSCO, Follett, Gardner's, Hertzberg, Ingram, Kobo, Library Direct, Mackin, Mindworks, Odilo, OverDrive, Everand

FREE multicultural ebooks, online SECRETS & lesson plans. Like our stories? Please comment online.

www.ingramcontent.com/pod-product-compliance
Lightning Source LLC
LaVergne TN
LVHW072102070426
835508LV00002B/229